Low Budget Bride's Planning Guide:

30 Thrifty Tips for Planning Your Dream Wedding

Forward

All brands, websites, etc. mentioned in this book are recommended from my personal experience and are not sponsored endorsements (though I would welcome those opportunities for my blog and future books).

Acknowledgements

This book would not have been possible without the help of a few special people.

1) Thank you to Jordan Schultz (my publisher) for presenting me with the opportunity to turn my blog concept into a book and being patient enough to wait a year for me to write it.

2) Thank you to Kelli Mahoney (my editor) for taking the time to read and edit multiple drafts of this book, as well as lending your professional insight on event planning.

3) Thank you to Olivia Corbett (my accountability partner) for supporting Low Budget Bride from the very beginning. Whether you are helping bring my creative ideas to life or making sure that I stay on top of my writing schedule, I am grateful for your consistent enthusiasm.

4) Thank you to Stephen Shackelford (the love of my life) for supporting all of my many endeavors, and loving this

frugal, detail oriented, low budget bride enough to marry her.

Summary

Nothing can ruin the bliss of an engagement like the sudden realization that you are about to plan the most expensive party you will ever through. Fear not, you can still have the wedding of your dreams, without spending a fortune. Let the Low Budget Bride teach you how to save thousands of dollars during the wedding planning process.

The idea of independently paying for such a large event was initially very intimidating. This book is based on my experiences and research during my own low budget wedding planning process. I have taken the best tips I learned and compiled them into a book so that other low budget brides can plan their weddings with a little less financial stress.

Here are a few of my favorite tips:
- Utilize ALL that is FREE
- Register for ANYTHING with Coupons
- Choose a Venue that Gives You Freedom
- Go Green

Table of Contents

Tip #1: Have a Longer Engagement

You don't have to get married within a year of getting engaged. In fact, you may want to consider doubling that amount of time for a low budget wedding. Allowing yourself to have a longer engagement not only means more time to plan, but also more time to earn and save money. Having the scheduling flexibility of a longer engagement will allow you to make more reasonable payments toward your expenses (Tip #28 will break this down further).

Whether you are intending to take on some debt, get financial help from family, pay for the majority of the wedding yourself, or any combination of the above, having time to save will be beneficial. One of the biggest topics couples fight over is money, so make sure you and your fiancé agree on the way(s) you will fund your wedding. After you determine your budget, figure out how much time you will need to achieve that budget, and create your savings plan accordingly (more on this in Tip #13).

You can also use your budget to determine the length of your engagement based on your financial capabilities. The first step is to develop as accurate of a budget as possible, which will be covered in a variety of tips later on. Next, determine what you can realistically save per month. Then divide your total budget by your estimated monthly savings to get the number of months it will take to reach your budget amount, and add three months (since some of your expenses will need to be paid in full three months in advance). You have just determined your engagement timeline.

Having a longer engagement gives you more time to shop for everything. You will not be rushed to pick a dress, venue, or vendor; you will have plenty of time to research and make educated decisions. You can also shop sales as they occur and stock up on things you will need (mason jars, picture frames, etc.) over time, rather than buying everything at once. Sure, you could max out a credit card buying everything you need and pay it off before your wedding, but then you will accrue interest charges, which takes away from your total budget. Making purchases over time will allow you to limit yourself to your monthly wedding spending budget, but still accumulate everything you need in time for your wedding.

Another factor to keep in mind when it comes to wedding shopping is your dress. If you choose not to buy off the rack, your dress could take anywhere from 4 to 9 months to be made and shipped back to your store. Plus, you will need additional time for alterations. To be safe, you should plan on at least 10 months between ordering your wedding dress and walking down the aisle in it. Even if you buy off the rack, shop second hand, or order from an online retailer, you should still give yourself at least a month for alterations and fittings to make sure the dress is tailored to your body.

A lot of money can be saved by going the Do-It-Yourself route when it comes to making your decorations, putting together your candy bar, and other DIY wedding projects., but these all require time. A longer engagement will give you more time to practice and complete anything you decide to make yourself. This will save you from the expense of having to hire somebody to complete those projects at the last minute if something goes wrong (Tip #20 will cover this in more detail).

Budgeting aside, coordinating a wedding is stressful. Do yourself a favor and give yourself at least a year (if not longer) to plan and organize your time and your budget. It will save you money (and keep you calmer) in the long run.

Tip #2: Invite Only the Most Important People

One of the most potentially stressful parts of planning a wedding is determining your guest list. While the names on your list may fluctuate during the initial planning stages, it is important to make a preliminary list in order to estimate your guest count. Have a discussion with your fiancé about whether or not you want to have an adult only wedding (eliminating younger guests will cut down your costs) and how many of your parents' friends you will invite (it is easy for this number to get out of hand). Both of these decisions can greatly impact the size of your guest count, which ultimately affects the size of your budget.

After setting some guidelines, the best way to begin is by making a general list of anyone and everyone you and your fiancé might want to invite. Consider the following categories of people during your brainstorming session: must-haves (your closest friends and family), extended family, your and your fiancé's additional friends, friends of your families, and co-workers. Then organize this list by creating A, B, and C sub-lists based on priority.

Here are a couple of questions to consider when dividing your list into A, B, and C categories:

1. Have you and/or your fiancé had a meal with this person in the last year or so?

- Yes: A List Material
- No: Possibly B or C List depending on the reason. If this person is family or a close friend that lives in another state, that could be an exception to this rule. If this person lives near you, but you have not gotten together in the last year, consider the reason(s) why. This will help separate the Bs from the Cs.

2. Do you and your fiancé both know this person?
   - Yes: A List Material
   - No: Possibly B or C List depending on the reason. The person you are marrying is obviously very important to you, so hopefully they have met most of the other important people in your life and vice versa. There will be exceptions to this rule, but consider how many exceptions you want to make. This day is about you AND your fiancé, so your guests should mostly be people who have known you throughout the course of your relationship. You can invite your parents' friends who have known you for a long time, but be sure to have a higher percentage of guests who are a part of both your and your finance's lives, as opposed to people who mostly know you separately.

Unless you have an unlimited budget (which, if you are reading this book, is probably not the case), you will most likely have to make some cuts to your guest list. This could be due to factors like your budget or the size of your venue. Either way, utilize your A, B, and C lists to figure out what will work best with the guest count you have set. There will almost always be people on your A list who cannot attend, so people from your B or C list may still get invited. Have an RSVP deadline that is early enough so you can still send your second round of invitations in a timely manner. No one should know where he/she ranked on your guest list, and it will be obvious if a last minute invitation is received.

Overall, remember that you are paying for each and every guest to attend your wedding. Pick the guests whose attendance will mean the most to you.

Etiquette Tip #1: Only send a Save-the-Date to guests who will definitely be invited to your wedding. You can always invite people who did not originally receive a Save-the-Date, but it is considered rude to send a Save-the-Date and then not invite that person to the actual wedding. Be sure to review and finalize your guest count based on your venue size, your budget calculations, and your A, B, C guest lists before sending out your Save-the-Dates.

Etiquette Tip #2: While it is optional to invite children or allow an "unattached" guest to bring a date, it is expected that you will invite the spouse, fiancé or live-in partner of everyone on your guest list (including your officiant). This rule of etiquette applies to low budget weddings too, so be sure to include these people in your guest count.

Tip #3: Utilize ALL that is FREE

You will be pleasantly surprised that a lot of great tools for wedding planning are at your disposal for FREE! That's right, FREE. I'll go into greater detail about wedding websites and ways to get coupons later (which are also FREE), but this tip is going to focus on utilizing all that is FREE within your network of people.

Here are a few simple ways you can utilize your network of friends and family. Ask yourself who you know and what services they can provide for your wedding. Do you know a photographer? A DJ? Someone who works for a wholesale florist? A baker who makes wedding cakes? Do you have connections that work in any of these wedding related industries? Contact anyone who could help (calling is better than emailing or texting, but work with the contact information you have) and ask. Even if the best they can do is get you a discount or complete their services at cost, asking for their help is FREE, and you may be surprised by how they can assist you.

Do you have friends or family members who recently got married? You might be able to borrow or buy (at a discount) some of their leftover wedding materials to help reduce your costs. Everything from mason jars to vases to pictures frames can be repurposed to fit your theme with changes as simple as switching out a ribbon color. Take good care of anything that is borrowed and return it in a timely manner. If they are giving you materials for FREE, be sure to send a handwritten thank you to show your appreciation for their generosity (though thank you cards are also strongly encouraged for everyone who helps with anything for your wedding).

Whether or not you decide to use an expensive photographer for your wedding day, consider having someone in your network of people do your engagement photos. Do you have a friend or family member who enjoys photography as a hobby? If you like previous photos that person has taken, ask if he/she would be willing to do your engagement photos. Worst case scenario, if the photos do not turn out the way you had hoped, you can always have them re-done professionally, but if they turn out well, you have just saved yourself at least a few hundred dollars. Plus, you have the added bonus of working with someone who knows you, which will make for a more natural, comfortable, and enjoyable photography experience.

Just about anyone can run a playlist off of a computer with the right technical set-up, so if you do not know someone who is a DJ, consider asking an outgoing friend to be your Master of Ceremonies and play the music for the evening. This will give you the flexibility to create your wedding playlist, ensuring the songs you want to hear make the cut and the songs you want to avoid do not (like "Celebration"). Be sure to meet with your MC in advance to go over your timeline for the evening. Discuss when specific songs need to be played (like "Single Ladies" for the bouquet toss), and when to announce events such as the cake cutting. Picking someone you know and trust for the task allows you to involve another friend in your wedding, while keeping your costs lower.

Tip #4: Don't be Afraid to Ask for Help

Weddings require a LOT of preparation. Sure, you can pay people to take care of everything for you, but if you want to keep your dream wedding low budget, don't be afraid to ask for help. In some cases, you may not even have to ask. You will be surprised at the number of people who WANT to help you in preparing for your big day.

Just as it is preferable to include friends and family in the big jobs for your big day (photographer, DJ, etc.), it is smart to have people who know you help with the finer details. This is also a great way to decide which family friends are bumped up from your B or C list. If you accept their help, be sure to add them to your final guest list. The people who are willing to volunteer their time and talents to help with your wedding are the people who should be part of your special day.

Here are some tasks that may require extra help:
1. Invitation Assembly
2. Making Decor (such as chair bows, centerpieces, signage)
3. DIY Projects
4. Day of Coordinator (someone who is super detail-oriented and organized)
5. Day of Set up (the more people you have, the less time you will need)

6. Cocktail Hour Hors o'devours serving
7. Reception Buffet serving
8. Cocktail Hour/Reception Bartending
9. Day of Clean up

Delegation is key to keeping your stress level low(er) when preparing for your wedding. If you have a friend who is a strong leader, have that person help coordinate the rest of your volunteers, particularly when it comes to day of set up. The last thing you want to worry about is whether or not the candy bar is organized correctly or if your tables have the right numbers on them. You can also prepare diagrams or do a practice set up ahead of time to ease your worries on the day of the wedding. Since these are your family and friends you can trust that they are going to put forth the extra effort to make your day as perfect as possible.

Etiquette Tip: Sometimes you will have to let people down. Though they have the best intentions, there may be people who want to help, but do not have the skills required to complete the tasks. In this situation, try to find alternative tasks for them, or politely let them know you have everything covered. For example, if someone has poor penmanship, but wants to help you address invitations, ask if they can be your "stamp placer" or "envelope sealer" instead. This will help you keep your sanity rather than stressing over returned invitations because the address could not be deciphered.

Tip #5: Designate a Wedding Email Address

This tip is mentioned early on because it will be a very valuable tool for you to have in conjunction with other tips mentioned later in this book. At some point you will be married and no longer interested in receiving a million emails per day about wedding photographers, venues, and couple's dance lessons (well maybe those ones are okay...date night idea, perhaps?). Having a separate email address for all wedding related email will alleviate the annoyance of deleting those unwanted messages on a daily basis for the rest of your life.

Creating a separate email address for wedding related content is a great way to keep all of that information organized as well, which is why it should be one of the first things you do. Do not, I repeat DO NOT sign up for ANYTHING until you have created this email address. In Tip #6, you will be encouraged to register for some of the best wedding planning resources, but they may send you an email every single day, so make sure you use your new email address. After you attend a bridal show, you will receive hundreds (no exaggeration) of emails from vendors, so use your wedding email address there as well.

If you choose to go green and digital for your RSVPS, guests may be replying to your wedding email address, so pick something that will be easy to understand. You will be using this email a lot during your wedding planning process, so it should be easy to remember too.

Here are some ideas:
1. Use both of your last names: yourlastnamefiance'slastnamewedding@gmail.com
2. Use the last name you will share: lastnamewedding@gmail.com
3. Use the first initial of each of your first names: AandBwedding@gmail.com

If you have a long last name and your fiancé has a long last name, you may want to reconsider including both last names in the email address, and go with one last name or your initials instead. Keep in mind that you will have to write out that email address when signing up with your vendors and venue or entering for FREEbies at the bridal show, so short and sweet will make life easier on your hand.

You are welcome to use whatever email platform you want, but there are a few reasons why Gmail is a great option. Using Gmail gives you the ability to utilize Google Docs and Sheets for tracking things like your budget, guest list, and day of schedule. It is also easy to share these docs and sheets with others for collaborative editing. Google even has a wedding dedicated website now (www.google.com/weddings) with FREE wedding planner templates. Visit the website and take a look at all of the other tools Google has to offer. If it saves you time and hassle, then it is definitely the way to go for your wedding email address and related documents.

Tip #6: Register for Wedding Websites and ANYTHING with Coupons!

While there are a lot of great wedding magazines that you can read for general tips as well as vendor and venue recommendations (Martha Stewart Weddings has more information than advertisements and is one of the least expensive), there are excellent ways to obtain that information for FREE as well.

Websites like the Knot and Wedding Wire are incredible sources of information. The Knot also has a magazine, but using their website is FREE! They will send you offers, coupons, and flash sale information, so be sure to use your designated wedding email address (Tip #5) when you register. The resources at your disposal when you utilize these websites include a large list of vendors and venues (with ratings and reviews), registry management, and wedding planning tools and tips. Additionally, you will be able to create your own wedding website, with a variety of features, including an RSVP function if you are going digital (Tip #24).

When creating your personal wedding website, you should include all of the important information for your guests. If you want to keep your wedding day details limited to only those invited to attend, use the password feature for privacy. This can be communicated to your guests on your save-the-date or wedding invitation.

Here are some suggested pages to add when developing your wedding website:
1. About Us
2. The Proposal
3. Wedding Party Who's Who
4. Wedding Day Event Details
5. Accommodations & Travel Tips
6. RSVP (if going digital)
7. Gift Registry

Additionally, you can use your website as a way to obtain information from your guests or communicate extra information to your guests. Sign up for a FREE account with Survey Monkey to create surveys for topics like guest accommodation needs (to help you estimate dates and number of rooms for your hotel room block) or beverage choices (to help you estimate how much you will need of different beverage types - both alcoholic and non-alcoholic). You can also create an FAQ page to address topics like bringing additional guests, appropriate attire, or religious traditions involved in your ceremony.

Though you will receive promotional emails as part of signing up with wedding planning websites, you should also register with websites that send coupons related to a variety of wedding essentials. Vistaprint and Snapfish send emails on a regular basis with discounts you can use on address labels, save-the-dates and invitations. For decor and party favors, Oriental Trading and Hobby Lobby have awesome coupons and a large selection of items for a variety of wedding needs. Also sign up with craft stores to get coupons for any potential DIY projects (Tip #20). Don't forget to use your designated wedding email address (Tip #5) when registering for coupons so they don't fill up your regular inbox.

Tip #7: Attend a Bridal Show

Bridal shows are a fantastic way to get FREEbies! By signing up with wedding planning websites and reading bridal magazines, you may even receive a FREE ticket or two to attend a show in your area. If you haven't received a FREE ticket, there are usually ticket promotions (especially buy one get one FREE) available if you purchase in advance. Even if you have to buy a ticket, the FREEbies you will receive generally outweigh the cost of admission. For starters, many bridal magazines are given away for FREE at the bridal shows (they normally cost anywhere from $4-$10 each). There are also food and beverage samples to try throughout the day and other FREEbies like skin care samples or fun pictures from the photo booths. You can even win prizes like FREE teeth whitening for your whole bridal party.

It is highly recommended that you print out address labels with all of your contact information (name, phone number, wedding email address, and mailing address) before attending the bridal show to save yourself the trouble of writing it down 100+ times in one afternoon. There will be a lot of vendors to meet, so this will save you time if you are trying to visit as many booths as possible. It also ensures that your contact information is legible and correct in case you win one of the many raffles you can enter at the event (you don't want to miss out on any FREEbies!).

You should also go into the bridal show with a mental outline (or a written one, if you prefer) of exactly what vendors you still need. Depending on where you are in the wedding planning process, you may be able to narrow down your search to specific vendor types such as photographers or bakeries. This will keep you focused on the priorities if you are unable to visit every booth that is participating in the show.

Also be sure to bring a camera or use the one on your smartphone. You will receive a lot of information (usually a big bag that will be filled with flyers and pamphlets throughout the day), but sometimes it is difficult to remember which vendors were your favorites. Take pictures of the vendors you like the most and anything they have displayed that particularly caught your interest. This will help you narrow down who to contact later on, especially if you are in the early stages of planning.

Since this type of event can be overwhelming and packed with people, limit the number of guests you bring with you. For the most part, the bride will be the only one able to enter drawings, so bringing a huge group of people will not increase your odds of winning. Whether you take your mom or your maid of honor, bring someone who is excited to attend the bridal show, will help you stay focused, likes tasting cake, and will pose for silly pictures in photo booths.

Tip #8: Cut Unnecessary Expenses in Your Current Budget

There are many ways to reduce the cost of your wedding celebration, but you also need to focus on your ability to save for the big day. Reducing your current expenses will allow you to put more money toward your wedding budget at a faster pace. This may require some sacrifices for both you and your fiancé, but they are only temporary.

> Gym Memberships: While being in shape for the big day may be important to you, there are plenty of ways to exercise without having to pay for costly gym memberships or personal training sessions. Group sessions are usually less expensive and a lot of exercise studios offer specials throughout the year on various classes. Search websites like Groupon to find discounted trial rates and experience something new every month, rather than paying for a membership somewhere. You can also explore the variety of videos on the internet for workouts you can do at home; there are ways to use everything from paper plates to soup cans as FREE home workout equipment. Lastly, go for a walk or run with your friends, fiancé or even the dog for FREE in your own community.

<u>Tanning, Nail, and Hair Appointments</u>: Beauty regiments are important, but reducing some of these costs for even half of your engagement can put a lot of money toward your wedding budget. If you want to be tan for your wedding, you don't need to start worrying about it until a month beforehand. Plus, you can lay out in the sun for FREE (just be safe and use SPF with those rays).

You may want your nails done for your wedding, but you can limit the number of professional manicures and pedicures you get beforehand by doing some (or all) of them yourself until the week of your wedding. You can even reduce the number of trips to the hair salon throughout your engagement to save for your wedding day. If you color your hair, consider picking a color that is low maintenance to maintain and only get your hair cut or trimmed as needed to keep it healthy.

<u>Date Nights and Meals Out</u>: While it is important to have date nights with your fiancé, they do not need to be expensive. Ideas for FREE date nights at home include finding a recipe to prepare together, watching a movie, playing a board game or video game, and going on a picnic. Whether you cook a meal at home together for date night or pack a lunch for work, reducing the number of times you go out to eat will also save you money. This includes $5

daily coffee drinks and happy hour on a weekly basis. Turn these habits into special occasions, and not only will you appreciate them more, but your wedding budget will grow.

Quick Fix Treatments: Forget the wraps, diet pills, or any other expensive "quick fix" treatments. Spending a fortune on special diets and weight loss pills to lose a few extra pounds in not worth the investment. Some of those "quick fix" weight loss treatments are essentially dehydrating your body or unhealthy for your metabolism, and the effects are only temporary. You already know that prepping your meals at home is less expensive, but it is also generally healthier too. If you make smart decisions about your nutrition and exercise regiment, then you won't need any of that "quick fix" stuff anyway. Your fiancé loves you the way you are, so take care of your body, and save your money for a nice pair of wedding shoes.

Cable/Satellite TV: Reality TV shows may be your guilty pleasure, but you can live without them for the next year, especially if it means saving the equivalent cost of 10-25 guests attending your wedding. Think about what percentage of your guest list that is. You can either reallocate your cable bill savings to the cost of 10 guests in your wedding budget, or have the opportunity to invite that many more guests to your wedding by reducing this one expense for one year. Though it may not be as convenient as watching your shows when they air or via your DVR, you can stream a lot of shows online as well as sign up for services like Netflix or Hulu Plus, which are a fraction of the cost of cable or satellite services, but still allow you to see your favorite shows.

Have a discussion with your fiancé about what expenses you are both willing to give up for the next year or so. It is important to make this decision together, especially if your finances are already combined. While making these sacrifices may only be temporary, they could also turn into a lifestyle change that affects your future finances together. If there is anything you really can't live without, call your service provider and ask about renegotiating your fee. They might be able to work with you if it will allow them to keep your business, and the extra money you save each month can go right into your wedding fund.

Tip #9: Determine What YOU Want the Most

Whether it's making decisions on wedding details or creating your gift registry, take time to discuss what things are most important to you... as in you + your fiancé = YOU. Keep the "YOU" formula in mind throughout all parts of the wedding planning process. While certain elements of the wedding might be more important to you than to your fiancé (and vice versa), you still need to listen to each other's thoughts and opinions to determine what you both want the most.

The Wedding Details: Every wedding is made up of components chosen by the bride and groom. No two weddings are exactly alike, just as no two couples are exactly alike. Take suggestions from friends, family, magazine articles, and other weddings you have attended, but when you finalize the details, your wedding should be unique to the two of you. In order to ensure this, you and your fiancé should make a list of the components that are most important to each of you and then compare.

Here are 10 topics to discuss (though you can definitely expand this list as you see fit):
- Theme/Color Scheme
- Location and Venue(s)
- Size of your Bridal Party (including who will be in it)

- Guest List (based on Tip #2)
- Menu
- Music
- Photography and Videography
- Officiant
- Paper vs Going Green
- Honeymoon

The Gift Registry: Every couple has different needs when they get married. Some couples may be living together for the first time, and others may have already merged their belongings. Each couple needs to evaluate what they have and decide what they need before making their gift registry. This is an opportunity to have nice dishes instead of your current set with missing pieces, or 800 thread count sheets instead of the mismatched ones you've had since college. Choose the items you need to help you start your new life together, and leave out the frivolities. What does this have to do with staying low budget? Well, if you get the items you need the most as gifts, then you won't have to buy them later on.

Additionally, there are ways to add your honeymoon to you gift registry. Compare different honeymoon funding websites and determine what best fits the honeymoon you are planning. For example, Disney and Sandals both have honeymoon registry programs specific to their properties. Research the different fees associated with each website to make sure you are getting the best deal overall. You can also book your honeymoon through a travel agent that offers payment plans; this allows your guests to call and make a payment toward your remaining balance as their gift to you.

Tip #10: Visit a Variety of Venues and Categorize Them

If you limit yourself to only traditional reception halls, you may miss out on some fun and less expensive options for your venue. When brainstorming the list of venues you want to visit, categorize them based on use (ceremony, reception or both), cost, and indoor vs outdoor. All of these categories will affect the way you develop your budget later on.

Ceremony only, reception only, or both
Having the ceremony and reception at the same venue will likely be the least expensive option, if that works with the needs for your dream wedding. For starters, you only have to pay one venue rental fee, if there is even a fee at all. There are also usually discounts on the overall price for a longer venue rental as opposed to a shorter one. If you have to rent equipment (tables, chairs, lighting, etc.), you will only need to rent one set and will be able to keep all of it at one location. You may need to adjust your set up from the ceremony to the reception, but the transition time will be shorter than driving from one venue to another.

Some circumstances may require you to have two venues. If you are planning on getting married in a church, you will most likely need a separate ceremony and reception location. You may also need a separate reception venue if your ceremony location is unable to accommodate dining space. Your cocktail hour can potentially be held at either the ceremony or reception venue, so keep this in mind when evaluating each location. For example, you could have your ceremony followed by a champagne toast at one venue and then dinner and the rest of your reception at another venue. As a courtesy to your guests, consider looking at reception venues near your ceremony venue or (if your budget allows) you can offer a shuttle service from either the ceremony to the reception or from the hotel hosting your room block to the reception. Not only is this a nice convenience, but guests will be able to avoid drinking and driving if you are serving alcohol at your reception.

Ranking 1 to 10 on the Cost Scale (1 = Free, 10 = Expensive)

The ranking is in reference to the base cost of a venue without any additional fees. For example, if the most you would want to spend on a venue is $10,000, then anything that amount or above would be a 10, a reception hall that costs $5,000 would be a 5, and utilizing someone's backyard for FREE would be a 1. This category will give you a starting point when it comes to narrowing down your top venues by price. There may be hardly any additional costs for a reception hall, while the backyard may have lots of extra costs ranging from renting a dance floor to covering the electric bill, so you will need to factor in the additional costs for all venues later on.

<u>Indoor vs Outdoor</u>
It is a common misconception that an outdoor wedding will be cheaper than an indoor one. In order to accurately compare, keep track of anything you would have to rent to use an outdoor venue, such as portable toilets and lighting. If there is a chance for rain, costs for a tent should be included in the budget as well (if the outdoor venue does not already have a covered space). There may also be fees for permits, noise restrictions, and a limited number of power sources, however, the base venue cost is usually less expensive (or FREE) for an outdoor venue verses an indoor venue. If your indoor venue rental only includes the venue itself and nothing additional, then some of the same additional charges may apply as they would for an outdoor venue. In the next section we will discuss the importance of knowing what is included and what costs are additional, which will be key when deciding between outdoor and indoor venue options.

Tip #11: Know What Is Included and What Is Optional For Each Venue

When comparing your budgets for different venue options (Tip #13), it is important to know what is included in your venue rental and what has an additional fee. Most venues will give you information during your site visit that breaks down different packages, as well as what can be added on. For example, the table cloths may be included, but the table runners and chair bows may cost extra. Clearly understanding what is included in your rental fee and what is optional will save you from surprise costs later on.

Here are some important questions to ask during your venue visit in order to accurately create your budget for that venue, as well as compare to other venue options:

1) Are set up and teardown included in my rental time block?
   • If not, what are the additional fees to have the venue provide set up and teardown?
   • Can I bring my own team to set up and teardown in lieu of paying the fee?
2) Can I come the night before or any earlier than my booked time the day of the wedding to pre-set my décor, wedding favors, table numbers, etc.?
3) What is the fee if I go over my booked rental time?
4) Is a ceremony rehearsal included in my rental fee?

5) Does the venue provide a wait staff?
   - If yes, are there any additional fees for servers, bartenders, etc.?
   - If no, are there requirements for bringing in my own wait staff?
6) Can I bring my own vendors?
   - If yes, are there any restrictions?
   - If no, which vendors does the venue work with?
     *This is especially important if you are booking a package deal with the venue as you may want to research their contracted vendors.
7) What technical capabilities and power sources does the venue have?
   - Note where the power sources are and how many are available, especially if you are planning to have a DJ and/or photo booth. This will help with your layout and is especially important for outdoor venues, since the number of outlets may be limited.
8) What equipment is included in the rental?
   - This includes tables, chairs, a bar, lighting equipment, etc.
   - If you are planning to play a video or slide show, make sure you know what capabilities and equipment the venue has available, as well as if there are additional fees to use it (price check against renting the equipment from somewhere else too).
9) Can I bring in my own alcohol?
   - If yes, what are the venue rules and regulations?
   - Is there a corkage fee?

- Is a certified/licensed/insured bartender required to serve alcohol?
10) Are any permits required?
  - This is especially important for outdoor venues, such as public parks.
11) What is the parking situation?
  - How many spaces are available?
  - Are there special loading areas for vendors?
12) Is there a place for the caterer to prep?
13) What is the deposit to book the venue?
14) Are payment plans available?
15) What is the cancellation policy?

Once you know what is included, what options cost extra, and the answers to the questions above, then you can evaluate the true cost of one venue verses another. If you know that one venue includes set up and teardown, but another does not, then factor in those costs when comparing the two for accuracy. If you have a venue that only allows you to use their contracted vendors, research the costs of those vendors and compare to any vendors you would select for a venue that allows you to bring in your own. A package may seem like a better deal at one venue, but when comparing the total package cost against bringing in your own vendors at another venue, you might find a surprising amount of savings.

Tip #12: Pick a Day Besides Saturday

Is picking a day besides Saturday considered unconventional? Maybe. Will it help your budget? Immensely!

Selecting a Friday or a Sunday is the first step to lowering your wedding costs, particularly in relation to your venue. On average, this change will save you a minimum of $1,000 on your venue rental. To take it a step further, compare the price of getting married on a weekend to getting married on a weekday. You may also be able to negotiate a longer rental time on a weekday (12 hours instead of only 6) and still keep your cost lower than a shorter, weekend wedding rental.

Additionally, consider getting married in the "off season" for your wedding location. This will vary from one location to another depending on the climate. For example, months like June, July and August tend to be discounted in the summer for a hot state like Arizona, whereas a state with a true winter season may offer discounts during colder months. When asking venues for information, be sure to inquire about "off season" discounts.

Etiquette Tip: Though you might get an awesome discount by choosing the "off season" for your venue, you still want to be courteous to your guests. Avoid picking dates during the holiday season, especially the middle to the end of December. You want people to be excited about attending your wedding, not stressed about travel or finances.

Combine an off season time of year with a weekday, and you are sure to save a ton on your venue! Plus, your vendors may offer weekday specials as well. If there is a vendor you are set on working with, make sure you know their scheduling options for weekdays before booking your venue for a specific date.

Some might wonder "is it reasonable to expect my friends and family to come to a wedding on a weekday?" The answer is "yes." It is highly unlikely that all of the guests you invite with RSVP "yes" anyway, even if you pick a Saturday, but the people who want to make your wedding a priority will find a way to be there, regardless of what day you pick. If you want to make the situation a little more convenient for your guests, look into holiday weekends as an option and get married on the Monday. Some venues may charge a different rate for a Monday on a holiday weekend, but for others it will be the same as their regular weekday pricing, saving you a lot of money on what is likely to be one of the most expensive expenses in your budget.

Tip #13: Create Budgets for Different Options

After you and your fiancé have determined what you each want most for your wedding (Tip #9), create and compare budgets for different options. Develop at least three budgets: one that is as cost effective as possible (aka: the frugal budget), one that encompasses anything and everything you could want (aka: the expensive budget), and one that falls somewhere in between, which includes elements from both the frugal and expensive budgets.

Additionally, you can create different budgets for different venue scenarios. This could be as simple as one budget per venue, or as complex as multiple budgets for each venue based on their pricing for different days of the week. Your venue cost (as well as some others) will vary based on which day of the week you get married, so once you narrow down your venue, you can create variations of your budget to reflect the costs for different days of the week. If you are considering an outdoor wedding, be sure to include all associated rental costs (tables, chairs, linens, restrooms, lighting, etc.).

You can apply this same concept to other budget elements, such as photography and videography. Create different budgets based on having only videography, only photography, and both. You can also do variations based on different packages offered by your photographer and videographer in regards to the amount of time they are shooting or the amount of product you receive from them.

Another element to consider is beverages. Will you have any alcohol? Just beer and wine? Hard liquor? Champagne toast? There are many combinations you can price out for this part of your budget. In order to help keep your budget as accurate as possible, use a drink calculator that creates estimates based on the number of guests and the length of your reception (Pinterest is a great place to search for an event beverage calculator).

Lastly, create budgets that compare different flower options for decor, bouquets, and boutonnieres. Flowers can end up being one of your biggest expenses, but there are ways to reduce the cost of the flowers you are using. Consider combining less expensive flowers with more expensive flowers to reduce the cost of your bouquets. You can also get creative and substitute flowers for seasonal alternatives, such as pinecones, berries or holly for a winter wedding (more on this in Tip #21).

Once you have determined which budget you will actually use, divide the total cost by the number of months you have left before the wedding to get an estimate for how much money you will need to save each month. Keep in mind, some vendors will require payment in full 60-90 days prior to the event, so you may need to have more money put away by that deadline to cover your costs. If the total number you need to save per month is intimidating, divide it in half and put that amount into your wedding fund every paycheck.

Tip #14: Use Your Venue Hours Wisely

Before booking your venue(s), have an idea of your timeline for the big day. Be sure to account for set up and teardown, as well as transition time, if you are going from one venue to another. It is easier to err on the side of more time than you need during your initial venue booking, rather than paying huge fees for going over your allotted time the day of your wedding. The last thing you want is to feel rushed at your reception, so depending on the type of reception you are having (just desserts vs a full dinner) plan for at least 3-5 hours of reception time.

Managing your set up and teardown time well is incredibly important. Some venues will set up tables, chairs, linens, etc. as part of your venue package, so make sure you know whether or not that is included, and if it will be completed before the start of your venue rental time. If you are responsible for set up and teardown, utilize your family and friends who have offered to help with your wedding (Tip #4). Know how many tables and chairs will need to be set up and ask the venue to give you a quote on approximately how much time it will take to assemble everything so you can plan accordingly. You don't want you volunteer team to be rushed or (worse) not have any time to get ready themselves before your ceremony.

Your volunteer team will be essential in preparing your venue(s) for the big day in many ways beyond general set up and teardown. This team can assist with tasks such as arranging your centerpieces, putting on your chair bows, and displaying your wedding favors. In order to help keep everyone on task, have a day of coordinator (which can also be a friend or family member who has offered to help) manage the prep the morning of your wedding. Work with your day of coordinator to create a timeline for the day, including all of the tasks that need to be completed during the set up.

If possible, have a "practice set up" before the wedding, so that everyone knows exactly what to do on that day. This can take place in someone's home and include basic elements of the set up to give you a good idea of how much time your volunteer team will need. Your practice set up will likely take longer than set up on the day of your wedding since it is everyone's first time tying the chair bows and arranging the centerpiece, but have someone keep time and see how well it matches your timeline. This will help determine if you have estimated a realistic amount of time for set up and allow you to adjust the schedule accordingly. You can also take pictures of your "practice set up" for your day of coordinator to bring the morning of your big day, so your volunteers have something to reference and you can get ready for your wedding worry free.

Tip #15: Choose a Venue that Gives You Freedom

Some venues offer all-inclusive packages. While this might seem like the easiest option, it may not be the most cost effective and could include things that you don't need. For example, you may already have a minister you know or a bakery you like or a friend who can DJ. To help keep your wedding low budget, it is imperative to research and compare all-inclusive venue packages to venues that give you the freedom to use your own caterer, florist, DJ, and so on.

One major budget saver is finding a venue that allows you to bring in your own food and beverages (F&B), preferably without a corkage fee or plating fee. As always, it is important to do you venue research and compare budgets for different options (Tip #13), because it could cost you more per person to include F&B in your venue package as opposed to using a separate caterer. By being able to pick your caterer, you will also have the freedom to choose exactly what you want for your menu, as well as accommodate guests who have kosher or allergy-specific needs. Ultimately the day should be about what YOU want, so you shouldn't be limited to only the few options provided by your venue.

If you are able to bring in your own food, you can choose to have your appetizers, main meal, and cake from whatever vendors you want. You can serve some homemade appetizers if your venue does not require that all food come from an approved establishment. If your venue does have that requirement, ordering your appetizers through a gourmet grocer could still be less expensive than a caterer or a restaurant. For your main course, compare pricing for a large party order from a restaurant versus a caterer. When you budget out the different options, you may be surprised by how much you will save going through a restaurant that includes salad and a side with their entrees, as opposed to paying for everything a la carte through a caterer.

When it comes to purchasing your beverages (including alcohol) one of the biggest cost savers is buying all of it wholesale. Generally, the cost of bringing in your own alcohol is less expensive than what a venue will charge you per bottle, per person or for an open bar. Of course this is contingent on your venue allowing you to bring in your own alcohol. Your venue may charge a corkage fee per bottle of alcohol that you provide, so be sure to include that in your budget. Your venue may also require you to have a licensed and insured bartender, which can cost an average of $200-$250. There are companies that hire out licensed and insured bartenders as well as a bar for them to serve at (if your venue does not have a bar included in the space you are renting). If you are hosting an outdoor reception in a public place, such as a park, research the local liquor license requirements at least a few months in advance, so you have time to apply for one as needed.

In addition to having freedom with food and beverages, consider a venue that allows you to choose the DJ, florist, and bakery you prefer. This will require more research on your part, but in the long run it could save you hundreds of dollars to mix and match the vendors that meet your needs rather than going with an all-inclusive package or a venue that requires you to use only their preferred vendors. All of the vendor research may be time consuming, but it is essential to keeping your costs as low as possible.

Tip #16: Serve Wine, Beer and Signature Cocktails

While a cash bar would definitely reduce your beverage budget, you should keep in mind that you are <u>hosting</u> an event. You wouldn't ask your friends and family to pay for beverages while attending a celebration at your house, so why would you expect them to pay for drinks at your wedding? That being said, you don't have to break the bank to provide alcohol for your reception.

As mentioned earlier, the first step to lowering your alcohol costs is finding a venue that will let you bring in your own alcohol. When purchasing your alcohol, go through wholesale vendors and keep an eye out for sales. You can also use a drink calculator (like the one mentioned in Tip #13) to estimate the number of bottles you will need to help with budget accuracy.

Another way to lower your alcohol costs is to limit what types of alcohol you are serving. Wine and beer can be the most cost effective and no mixers are required. You can offer a few different types of each (in addition to your non-alcoholic options), so there are a variety of choices for your guests. If you want to serve hard liquor, create one or two signature drinks; you can even have a "bride's favorite" and a "groom's favorite" to keep it tied to the wedding. This will not only make your bartender's job a little easier, but your budgeting will also be less complicated by only having to create estimates for a few types of alcohol and limited mixers.

In addition to offering wine, beer, and maybe some signature drinks, you also have the option to include champagne. Since good champagne can be costly, limit it to toasting instead of serving it at the bar. Alternatively, you can use sparkling cider for toasting or even have guests toast with whatever they are already drinking. This also eliminates the potentially awkward situation of champagne being offered to guests who are underage or who choose not drink.

You want to make sure that guests who are not of age, or who chose not to drink alcohol, still have beverage options. When adding in the beverage section of your budget, include water, non-alcoholic beverages, and mixers (if applicable). Keep an eye out for sales on bottled water and soft drinks, so you can stock up when they are the cheapest. Generic bottled water is usually less expensive than name brands, and if you get a really good deal on the generic water, you can still make it look fancy by ordering custom labels from Etsy for the same total price (or less) than buying name brand water.

Tip #17: Compare Catering Options

For this tip, we will be referencing Tip #13 and Tip #14, where we discussed creating budgets for different options and the perks of a venue that allows you to select your own caterer. In order to make sure that choosing your own caterer is less expensive than going with an all-inclusive package, you will need to create different budgets to compare your options.

The first step is to narrow down which caterers you like. Attending bridal shows and venue open houses will give you the opportunity to sample local caterers. Be sure to make notes on their business cards or menus to help you remember what you specifically liked when you review them at home. Additionally, check with your favorite restaurants to see if they offer large party/group catering. Chain restaurants may have packages that include a salad, entree, and main dish for half the price of a caterer. Also look into regular and gourmet grocers who offer catering.

Once you have determined which caterers and restaurants are your favorite, work them into your budgets for comparison. Get pricing for family style, buffet style, and plated meals to calculate which will give you the best value. Serving the meal family style may give you the lowest per person cost from one caterer, while serving the meal buffet style might be a better value from a different caterer.

You can also mix and match options from different caterers and restaurants to find the best combined per person cost for your budget. For example, you might have the gourmet grocer catering department prepare some of your appetizers, but use a restaurants salad, entree, and side combo for your main menu. Knowing the differences between your catering options can also help you with negotiating (Tip #27) if your preference would be to use the same caterer for everything.

Another option is to prepare some of your menu at home (if your venue allows this). Serving homemade appetizers during your cocktail hour has multiple advantages. You can showcase favorite family recipes, such as one of your mom's specialties or a dish that has been in the family for years. For added personalization, have a couple dishes from each side of the family displayed with the other appetizers and include a card that explains the origin of the family dish. You can also cut costs by prepping your own fruit, cheese, and cracker trays. The cost to prepare these appetizers on your own verses purchasing them pre-made is usually half or less. Gather some of your volunteers and bridesmaids to put these together the day before or morning of the wedding.

It is important to serve quality food to your guests, but you should be able to keep your costs at approximately $15-$20 per person if you research and budget effectively. That is at least half of what some venues will charge with their packages. The food will (hopefully) not be what your guests remember most about your wedding, so as long as it tastes good, they will be satisfied.

Tip #18: Try Alternatives to Traditional Wedding Cake

Even though the tradition of a wedding cake dates all the way back to the days of Ancient Rome (thanks Wikipedia), you are by no means obligated to stick with it, especially if you can choose an alternative that better suits your budget and the feel of your wedding.

Here are four alternatives to a traditional wedding cake:

Option #1: Fake Cake and Sheet Cake

"Fake Cakes" are a new trend in the wedding industry. They can be rented or bought, but either way it will save you hundreds of dollars compared to a traditional wedding cake. Some fake cake vendors make the top layer edible and others work in just one edible slice to enhance the illusion. After you and your groom have cut the edible part of the fake cake for yourselves, it can be brought to the kitchen, and then slices of sheet cake can be brought out and served to your guests. Sheet cake will cost you an average of 75 cents to $1 per person, whereas traditional wedding cake usually runs closer to $4-$6 per person.

Option #2: Dessert Bar

Having a dessert bar gives you the opportunity to have multiple sweet options and will generally be less expensive than a wedding cake, depending on what you incorporate. There are no rules to a dessert bar (other than it should contain dessert), so get as creative as you want with the variety of desserts you offer. In lieu of the traditional cake cutting/serving, you and your spouse can feed each other ANY kind of dessert you want, which is great if either or both of you are not fans of cake. This option also allows you to include desserts that meet different dietary needs or requests: vegan, kosher, sugar-free, gluten-free, or dairy-free. Just be sure to create signage so everyone knows what each item is and if it is designated to meet one of those needs.

Option #3: Small Decorative Cake

You may really want to have a traditional wedding cake to display - especially so you can cut the top layer to ~~shove in your new spouse's face~~ feed to your new spouse - but you don't have enough money in your budget for a $500+ beautifully decorated wedding cake. Instead of splurging on a large decorated cake, have an elaborate smaller cake created. It can be small enough for just the two of you, or maybe a little bigger, but not as big as would be needed to feed your entire guest list. When it comes time bring the cake out for your guests, serve slices of a sheet cake (like in option #1), and add whatever slices are left from you small cake to the sheet cake slices, or to a dessert bar (like in option #2).

Option #4: Small Decorative Cake with Cupcakes

Incorporating cupcakes is a great way to give your small cake a fuller look while still saving money, however, the key to keeping this option low budget depends on the type of cupcakes you order. For example, gourmet cupcakes can cost almost as much (if not the same) as a wedding cake. Price check the combination of cupcakes and a small decorative cake versus a larger decorative cake before making a final decision.

Tip #19: Get Inspiration and Organization from Pinterest

Pinterest, though a newer tool for brides, is invaluable in its organization and inspiration capabilities. It is FREE to register for an account and it's easy to use.

Inspiration (aka: "Pinspiration):

> Though looking at wedding magazines and attending bridal shows can give you a plethora of great ideas, Pinterest is a fun and FREE resource available to any bride. Many women create wedding themed boards on Pinterest even before they are engaged, but if you haven't done so yet, now is the time. It may seem overwhelming at first, but Pinterest is a great way to explore different themes and color schemes, as well as research topics like bridal gowns, bridesmaid dresses, wedding hairstyles, and bouquet arrangements.
>
> In addition to pinning things for you big day, you can also research ideas for other wedding related events, such as your engagement photo session, bachelorette party and bridal shower. There are even great suggestions for ways to ask your bridesmaids to be part of your big day. Not only can you pin the pictures of each idea to your board, but most of them have a link to the products or blog

tutorials related to each pin for future reference. This will come in handy for any DIY projects (Tip #20) you pin, making it easy to find the instructions for the crafts later on, since they will be linked to the picture.

Organization:

As you begin to find ideas you like, add them to a board dedicated to your wedding. If you want to keep them a secret, make your wedding board private, or allow only select Pinterest users to see and pin to the board (e.g. your bridesmaids, Mother-of-the-Bride, and Mother-of-the-Groom). You can also create a separate board for your bridesmaids to collectively share ideas as a group. This is particularly helpful for planning the bachelorette party and bridal shower.

Since there are a lot of great suggestions for both engagement and wedding day photo shoots, create a board dedicated to photography as well. Having ideas going into either of those photography sessions will ensure that you take pictures in the poses you really like. It will also keep your sessions focused and organized, which will help you maximize the number of photos taken during your limited time with the photographer.

You can have up to 500 boards on your Pinterest account, so feel free to break each one down into very specific categories, depending on how you like to organize. If you find an idea you like on another website, you can also pin that to one of your boards, using the little Pinterest button that can be added to your browser. Pinterest allows you to have 200,000 pins, so don't worry if you feel like you are getting carried away with pinning. If you somehow manage to max out your 200,000 pins, just create another account with your wedding email address.

Tip #20: Practice your DIY (Do It Yourself) Projects

With the help of Pinterest (Tip #19), DIY - **Do It Yourself** - wedding projects are easy to find. There are many blogs and articles available for creating pretty much anything you can think of for your wedding day. DIY projects can potentially save you a lot of money on everything from arranging your own flowers to making your escort cards to putting together your reception centerpieces.

Before buying supplies for your DIY projects, compare the estimated cost of the project to the cost of buying the final product to make sure DIY is truly the more budget friendly way to go. If it is, then also add 10% to your estimated cost when figuring it into your budget, just in case you need extra supplies (better to over-estimate and end up with extra money in your budget, than the other way around).

Also be sure to check with your venue about your DIY projects before purchasing supplies that you may not be able to use for anything else. Some venues have specific rules that must be followed, such as requiring a fire permit for live candles. It'll be easier to shop for battery powered fake candles if you know this in advance, rather than trying to find them hours before your reception.

DIY can help your budget significantly, however, you still want to do a quality job, and that can be a challenge if you do not give yourself enough time (Tip #1). Once you have narrowed down what elements of the wedding you will create yourself, start by practicing the project on a small scale.

Here are a few reasons why you should give each DIY project a trial run:

1) To make sure you can successfully DIY and be satisfied with the results.

    Some projects may not be as simple as a blog post makes them seem (for examples, just search "Pinterest fail" on Google). Knowing far enough in advance to have a backup plan will save you from stressing over the project close to your wedding day. If you have friends or family who are particularly crafty and have offered to help with your wedding (Tip #4), be sure to recruit them for assistance, especially if they have experience with the project you are attempting. Knowledgeable craft partners will not only help your project turn out better, but may also save you stress and wasted supplies.

2) To determine the actual amount of time it will take to complete the project.

No bride wants to stay up until 2AM the night before her wedding decorating those escort cards. By practicing your projects in advance, you will not only work through any kinks, but you will also have a better idea of how much time it actually takes to complete each project. Having knowledgeable assistance can help here too because they may have an even easier and/or less expensive way to complete the DIY project than the instructions you found. If you run out of time to DIY, it will be a hard hit to your budget to rush order something from a vendor, so good planning and time management is also key.

3) To figure out exactly what you will need in supplies per project.

Save yourself potential frustration and buy a minimal amount of extra supplies the first time you attempt a new DIY project, just in case you make a mistake. Since you will likely be doing this project again, the supplies will not go to waste, but you will have room for error the first time you try it out. Once you have successfully completed the project, multiply what you actually needed in supplies for your practice run by how many versions of that same project you need to create for your wedding to calculate what additional supplies you need to buy, so that you don't over spend. Only open supply packages as you need them to complete your projects, and be sure to keep all of your receipts, so you can return any unopened/unused supplies after you are completely finished with the project.

When gathering your supplies, shop smart to keep your costs low. Make your supply list early on so you can watch for sales and search for the store/vendor that has the best deal. Take a trip to the dollar store before buying supplies anywhere else. If the quality is not up to your standards, then you can always shop another retailer, but you may be surprised at what you find. Potential supplies found at the dollar store include tissue paper, balloons, favor boxes/bags, lights, fake candles, real candles, candle holders, fake flowers, vases, and frames. You can also search party supply wholesalers, especially for anything you need to buy in bulk. For anything that needs to purchased from a regular retailer, find coupons (Tip #6) and shop sales.

Tip #21: Select Flowers Smartly

Flowers can be one of the most expensive categories for a wedding budget, but fortunately there are a lot of ways to customize how you use them. Start by making a list of all the ways you may want to include flowers in your big day, then re-sort your list by ranking of most to least important. This gives you an organized visual to refer to once you start getting your floral estimates. It will be easier to see where you may want to eliminate flowers if you have already decided on the most/least important ways to include them.

Purchasing your flowers from a wholesale florist and arranging them yourself can be a huge cost saver, but like any other DIY wedding project (Tip #20), make a practice arrangement to determine if you are satisfied with what you can create on your own. You also want to figure out how much time it will take to make your bouquets, centerpieces, and boutonnieres to see if the DIY savings are worth the time required to put them together. These factors will help you decide if you should consult a florist for some or all of your floral needs.

Knowing what flowers will be in season at the time of your wedding is important, whether or not you are putting together your own arrangements. Flowers that are in season can be less expensive than flowers that are not in season, regardless of shopping wholesale or with a florist. Flowers will also typically last longer if they are in season, especially ones that are grown locally. If the types of flowers you want to use are not in season, you can still reduce your costs by using less of those flowers in combination with flowers that are in season or are less expensive.

If you ultimately decide to order through a florist, here are some other ways you can still reduce your costs:

1) Request a detailed breakdown of the florist's fees
   You may be able to eliminate some add-on costs for things that you don't need (filler flowers, ribbons, etc.), if you know exactly what is included. Also inquire about fees related to pick-up verses delivery. While delivery may be more convenient, having one of your friend/family volunteers pick up your flowers and deliver them to your venue(s) may cut your flower costs significantly (Tip #4).

2) Re-purpose flowers from the ceremony for the reception
   If you are displaying flowers at your ceremony location, utilize them at your reception too. Depending on the size of an arrangement, you may be able to use it as a centerpiece or in other areas of your reception site. You can also use the

bridesmaids' bouquets as centerpieces, since they won't need to hold them for the reception.

3) Mix expensive flowers with less expensive flowers

Combining the more expensive/not in season flowers with less expensive/in season flowers allows you to use the ones you want the most, while still staying within your budget. You can also limit the use of more expensive flowers to only arrangements that matter the most to you, such as your bouquet. Then use large amounts of less expensive flowers - like daisies and carnations - in the same color to create arrangements that look fuller and pop, while keeping your costs low.

4) Use some flower alternatives

After doing your research, if fake flowers are more cost effective that real flowers, use those for your centerpieces and order just your bouquets and boutonnieres through the florist. You can also incorporate things found in nature that are less expensive than traditional flowers, but bring uniqueness to your boutonnieres and bouquets. For example, couples who are fans of Dr. Who might include a stalk of celery in the groom's boutonniere. Another possibility is incorporating seasonal accents - like pinecones in the winter - that work well with your wedding theme. Broach bouquets are another pretty and elegant alternative for the bride and bridesmaids, however, they can be equal to the expense of flowers, so research the cost of ordering them from different vendors or make it a DIY project.

5) Limit the number of flowers you are using overall
Think outside the box and your creativity might lead you to something more personal to your wedding and theme. Every centerpiece does not need to include flowers and groomsmen can sport pocket squares instead of boutonnieres. Create centerpieces with other types of decor such as seasonal fruit, succulents, candles, lanterns and picture frames, so you can save the fresh flowers for where you feel they are most important.

Tip #22: Compare Photography Options

You want to do something to capture memories on your big day, but having a photographer, videographer, and photo booth can get pretty expensive. There are so many vendors and options that this can also become one of the most overwhelming decisions in wedding planning. For <u>each</u> photography category, research vendors (online, at bridal shows, or by recommendations from people you know), make a list of your favorites, and then narrow them down to a list of three vendors (similar to Tip #13):

1.   A vendor that is close to your maximum budget for photography
2.   A vendor that is the least expensive
3.   A vendor that is somewhere in the middle.

If you really like the work of a vendor that is over your budget but reasonably close to it, you might be able to negotiate with them (more about that in Tip #27), but be realistic in your negotiation expectations. Fees that are a few hundred dollars over your budget are going to be easier to negotiate than $1,000 or more over budget.

Now that you have your list of 9 vendors (3 for each category), think about the benefits of having a photographer, videographer and photo booth at your wedding, and decide what you want from your wedding photography. You may ultimately decide that you don't need all three or that one is more important than the others. These decisions will help you appropriately re-allocate the funds in the photography section of your budget. This may give you the ability to choose the more expensive photographer by skipping the photo booth, or have both a photographer and videographer by selecting a photography package with less features.

Here are some ideas to get you started on your photography decision making:

- Photographer
    Benefits:
    1. You will have professional photos from your wedding day.
    2. You will have tangible access to memories from you wedding.
    3. A photographer can shoot at better angles for your ceremony than guests who are seated in rows.
    4. If you have two photographers, they can capture a wider spectrum of your day (e.g. one can take photos of the bride and bridesmaids getting ready while the other takes photos of the groom and groomsmen; one can take photos of the bridal party between the ceremony and the reception, while the other can photograph the cocktail hour), which will

allow you to see moments that you would have otherwise missed.
5. You will have high-resolution candid photos from your reception in addition to the traditionally posed photos between your ceremony and cocktail hour.

Ways to Reduce Cost:
1. Have one photographer instead of two. Your guests will be happy to share the photos they take with you, so you will still end up with plenty of pictures. You can even create a photo sharing site for FREE on websites like Shutterfly, where guests can upload and tag photos of your wedding in one place.
2. Cut some or all pre-ceremony photos. Your bridesmaids and groomsmen can help capture some of these moments while you are getting ready.
3. Don't have a photographer for your whole reception. Estimate the amount of time needed for the big moments (like the bouquet toss and your first dance), pictures with each table, and some reception dancing. Use that approximation to schedule the cut off time for your photographer(s), because let's be honest... sweat is not the most attractive thing to see in photos once the dancing has begun.

4. Learn about all of the packages your photographer offers and how that compares to your photography needs. Attempt to negotiate out any of the features you don't need. Also keep in mind the savings of any promotions they offer, such as a FREE engagement session or boudoir shoot with the purchase of a wedding package.
5. Hire a photographer who will let you pay a fee for printing rights or already includes them in their packages. This will give you unlimited opportunity to print your photos without having to pay high prices for prints from your photographer.

- Videographer
     Benefits:
     1. Video can capture both visual and audio of important moments like your vows or your best man's speech, whereas photos alone cannot.
     2. You can have a video guest book - where guests record messages to the bride and groom upon entering the reception - as an alternative to a signature guest book.
     3. You can watch the recording of your wedding day in the future to remember it in great detail, almost like reliving it again.

4. You can share your wedding day with people who could not attend or even your future children.

Ways to Reduce Cost:
1. If you have a photographer covering the bridal party getting ready, have your videographer start at the ceremony.
2. You can also set your contracted hours with the videographer just long enough to film the important parts of the reception (bridal party entrance, speeches, first dance, etc.) and end before the late night drunken dancing begins.
3. If there is a discount to order multiple copies of your wedding video, see if any family members want a copy, and split the cost evenly with them (you know at least your mom is going to want one).

• Photo Booth
    Benefits:
    1. Your guests will receive a tangible memory to take home.
    2. A copy of each photo strip can be placed in an album for you and signed by guests, in lieu of traditional guestbook.
    3. It gives your guests a form of entertainment during the cocktail hour and reception.

4. Photo booths allow you and your guests to take some fun pictures that show your personalities in a contrasting way to the traditional wedding photos you posed for earlier.

Ways to Reduce Cost:
1. Contract your photo booth vendor for a limited number of hours. If guests know there is a time limit and they want a chance to take some goofy pictures home, they will make it a priority to hop in the photo booth before it's too late.
2. Create your own photo booth! If you are already hiring a photographer (or two) designate part of your cocktail hour or reception time for the photo booth. You can make your own backdrop for under $25 and buy or make some props to go with it. You could even let guests take their own photos with the backdrop and props you provide (though you may want to assign someone to manage the photo booth area, like one of your volunteers from Tip #4).
3. Put disposable cameras on the reception tables and let your guests capture candid and silly photos on those. When you get them developed, order extra copies to include when you send thank you notes to your guests. You

can also order a digital copy of the prints to post on social media, and reprint them without needing permission from the original photographer (which can cut down the amount of pictures you will need to order from your professional photographer too).

In addition to whatever combination of photography, videography, and photo booth you choose, there are also photo sharing apps for smartphones that can be used to help capture your day. A lot of them are FREE and come with a variety of features (including photo sharing from other wedding events like your Bridal Shower). Invite guests to join the app and share their photos from your wedding events in one place. This will give you access to even more photos from your big day, without any extra cost. You can also create a signature hashtag for your wedding, which guests can include when they post pictures on social media. This will make it easier for you to find those photos and posts on apps like Instagram.

Tip #23: Shop Around Before Ordering Your Invitations

To get the best price, shop around before ordering your save-the-dates, invitations, response cards, etc. This is where registering for coupons comes in handy (Tip #6). If you sign up for the FREE coupon mailing lists from multiple vendors early on, you will have an idea of the types of coupons and offers they send out, as well as how frequently they are available. Be sure to use your wedding email address (Tip #5) so your personal email isn't loaded with promotions every day of the week. Compare pricing and factor in those coupons to figure out the best deal.

Though you are trying to keep costs low, you also want to feel proud of the invitations you are sending out. If possible, get a preview of what your invitations will look like before you order them. Some companies will send you a FREE sample pack of their invitations just for signing up on their website. You can also ask friends and family for references based on the invitation vendor they used. They may have a copy of their invitation for you to look over, and could even still be receiving email coupons from that vendor.

If you have read even one wedding magazine, you have noticed the abundance of advertisements from companies that design wedding stationary (basically on every other page). While some of these companies may offer great deals, don't forget to check out other printing vendors too, especially if you want to include photos on your save-the-dates. You may even be able to get nice save-the-date magnets from one vendor for the same price as paper ones from another. Though they may not be the first to come to mind, websites like Vistaprint, Snapfish and Costco have great design choices, low costs, and additional offers/discounts, which will help you stay within your budget. Don't forget to add these vendors to your list of places to sign up for coupons once you make your wedding email address.

There are also graphic design vendors who will create a personalized wedding suite for you that you can print yourself. For this option, be sure to calculate the cost of paper and ink in addition to the graphic design fee to accurately compare with the price of ordering from a different vendor. If you end up going digital with your save-the-dates and invitations, having a custom designed suite could be a fun and unique way to use that part of your budget, while still keeping costs lower. You'll learn more about the benefits of going digital in the next section (Tip #24).

Before you order anything that will need to be mailed, determine the required amount of postage to send it. This cost will vary depending on the size, shape, and weight of what you are sending. Research your postage costs in advance based on the dimensions of the products you are planning to order. You can even bring the invitation sample to the post office for verification. Combine the costs of postage and invitations to get the most accurate estimate for your budget.

Tip #24: Go Green

In the digital age, there is now a cost-effective way to communicate wedding information to your guests, while also benefiting the environment by using less resources. It's called "Going Green." Couples have the option to "Go Green" with some or all of their wedding communication; this can be done in conjunction with their wedding website. Since people feel special when they receive something like a personal invitation (a nice break from bills and junk mail), you can send either your save-the-dates or invitations in the mail, and "Go Green" with everything else.

If you email your save-the-dates and invitations, or provide details to your guests through a wedding website, you want your digital communication to look as nice as a formal invitation. As mentioned in Tip #23, you could use some of the money you are saving on printing and shipping to hire a graphic artist to design a custom theme for your save-the-dates, invitations, response cards, and even your website. You can also make a detailed wedding website that is as beautiful as an invitation, but much less expensive (and it won't get lost in the mail). If those options are still above your budget, there are FREE and inexpensive alternatives you can use as well.

When you sign up with websites such as the Knot or Wedding Wire, a FREE personal wedding website is included with your FREE membership. You will have to pay a fee if you want a specific domain name, but even that cost is usually pretty reasonable. You can choose from many different templates and themes, as well as additional features to customize your website. It can be password protected, so only invited guests have access to specific details. There is even an option to have guests RSVP through your website, which eliminates the cost of response cards and postage, as well as the possibility of them getting lost in the mail. The RSVP information collected can then be used to create your seating chart on the backend of your website, without having to map it all out on paper.

If you want to take your wedding website to the next level, you can purchase a professional, custom website and coordinating app. For example, appycouple.com charges a $35 one-time fee for this type of service, and your account is active as long as you need it. If your guests have all the weddings details on an app where they can also submit their RSVPs, you eliminate the need for invitations and response cards. You can also include other pre-wedding events on the website and app, such as your bridal shower or rehearsal dinner. This reduces the need to print and mail those invitations, plus your guests can RSVP for them through the app too. In addition to all of the digital communication, there are other benefits to having an app, including a feature where guests can take pictures. Photos taken through the app are automatically saved to your gallery, so you have a copy of them as well.

The only catch with "Going Green" is there may be people on your guests list who are not savvy when it comes to apps, email, or the internet in general. In cases like this, you may need to order some printed save-the-dates, invitations and response cards. On websites like Snapfish you can order a set of invitations for under $20 (not including all of their other discount offers), or design a custom card for $2.50, which could be made to look like an invitation. These costs are still significantly lower than printing everything, and you are putting less waste into the environment by reducing the amount of paper you are using. You can encourage your guests to recycle the printed invitations after the wedding in support of your "Go Green" efforts, but don't get too upset if they plan on keeping them for a scrapbook.

Tip #25: Pick Practical Wedding Favors

Wedding favors are a nice way to thank your guests for attending your big day. While some couples go above and beyond with their favors, there are many options you can choose that will keep your favor budget under $2-$3 per person.

When it comes to choosing favors for any event, picking something edible is always a great decision because most people like treats. There are many companies that specialize in custom desserts, but you'll definitely want to look for deals on these to stay low budget. You can add a personalized label around a box of tiny macaroons, print an edible image directly onto a sugar cookie, or put your picture on m&ms that match your wedding color scheme. To keep your costs even lower, skip the personalization and use a colored treat box or cellophane bag with a pretty ribbon to keep your wedding favors contained in a classy way.

Candy and popcorn bars have become a trendy new way of distributing wedding favors. This allows your guests to choose exactly what they want. You can provide as many varieties of popcorn or candy (or both) as you want, and guests can fill a designated box or bag with their favorites. You can also accommodate food allergies and sensitivities with this type of favor by providing (and labeling) options that are gluten-free, nut-free, etc., so your guests feel comfortable taking home their treats. There are a lot of candy wholesale retailers, so this is another task that will require research to stay low budget, but what could be more fun than researching candy?

If you want to choose something that will last longer than the yummy favors mentioned above, shop the deals you are receiving in your wedding email (Tips #5 & #6). For example, the Knot sends out regular emails with great bargains on a variety of good wedding favor options. You can find things like custom shot glasses (under $2 each), heart-shaped wine stoppers (under $3 each), or personalized stemless wineglasses (under $2 each). Overall, if you are not going the edible route, pick something your guests might actual use beyond your wedding day so you aren't wasting your money. Even a favor that is only $1 per piece is still $100 down the drain if 100 people throw it away when they get home.

Tip #26: Consider Non-traditional and Less Expensive Attire Options

Though there may be traditional expectations, there is a lot of flexibility in what you can choose for your wedding attire and accessories. Nowadays it is common for bridesmaids to wear all different styles of dresses; they may also be in a coordinating color scheme, but not necessarily in the exact same color. Footwear is no longer limited to dress shoes and heels. A veil is not the only acceptable headpiece for the bride. Some brides may even wear a color other than traditional white or ivory. When deciding on attire for you, your fiancé, and your bridal party, open your mind to the many options available. You may find that choosing something non-traditional is not only more personal and fun, but also budget-friendly.

While many ladies dream of buying a designer gown, especially one made specifically for the bride, this is often the most expensive option for purchasing your wedding dress. You may be surprised at what you can find off the rack or at sample sales, so definitely check those out first. There are also consignment stores and websites that re-sell wedding dresses, which are sometimes still new with the tags attached. Repurposing a family member's gown is a great way to incorporate "something borrowed" while making it your own, and only paying for alterations instead of buying a new dress. Overall, you want to feel beautiful in your wedding dress, so if you decide to order a designer gown (which can still cost less than $1,000 and may fit fine into your budget), there are other ways to reduce your expenses in regards to attire.

Once you decide on a dress, start browsing ideas for hairstyles and accessories. In addition to the traditional veil, flower crowns have become a beautiful new trend, and they can be arranged in an endless number of ways. There are also a wide variety of tiaras and barrettes to choose from, depending on the hairstyle you select, and Etsy has shops where you can order custom ones too. You could also make your own veil, which may be significantly less expensive than buying one, but be sure to follow all of the previous recommendations for DIY projects (Tip #20). Lastly, your hair accessory is another great way to use a "something borrowed" item, which would be the least expensive of all because it's FREE.

There are so many options when it comes to your shoe choices, but with patience, research, and bargain shopping, you can find the perfect pair without overspending your budget. If the $800 Louboutins you love are just not attainable, search for similar styles by less expensive designers. Shop major sale days to get the best deals at department stores, and browse discount stores like Nordstrom Rack and DSW for a stylish designer shoe at a more affordable price. You can even opt for a pair of cowboy boots, Converse (their website has lots of customizable options), or TOMS (they even have a "wedding" section), which are fun and affordable for the whole bridal party.

Just remember, the most important factor when selecting your wedding shoes - whether they are $40 Converse or $800 Louboutins - should be comfort. Sure, you may want footwear that fits a variety of other adjectives (cute, fun, chic, lacy, satin, flat, high, etc.), but they won't seem like the "perfect" shoe when your feet are dying and the reception hasn't even started yet. If your budget allows, you can always have a pair of "reception shoes" to wear if your "ceremony shoes" will only remain comfortable for a few hours.

Even though the focus of this book is on your budget, you should keep in mind the budget of your bridal party as well. By agreeing to be part of your big day, they are also committing to the attire you select for them to wear, however, be reasonable in your requests. They may need time to budget too, so once you have an estimate for their attire (including shoes), let them know. For the groomsmen, consider having them buy a suit they can re-use instead of renting a tux that is more expensive and has to returned within 48 hours. If you find a bridesmaid dress style you really like, but it's expensive, see if another designer or retailer carries something similar. If you are open to your bridesmaids wearing different dresses in the same color/color scheme, let them choose their own dress (with your approval) that fits in their price range. It is also a nice gesture to pick a color and/or style they could realistically wear again, but not an obligation.

Tip #27: Negotiate Negotiate Negotiate

You deserve to have your dream wedding at the lowest, reasonable price, but you are going to have to work for it. One of the biggest tools to lowering your costs is negotiating with your vendors. Be firm in your negotiations, but remember to be polite as well. Vendors are not just business owners; they are people too. If done correctly, a negotiation will leave both parties content without anyone feeling bullied.

As mentioned in many other tips in this book, it is important to thoroughly research your options before making a decision. This is especially true prior to negotiating with your top vendor, because the more knowledge you have of competitors' prices, the easier it will be to determine what is reasonable for the services you need. Having the price breakdown from other comparable vendors will also give you leverage by being able to show your top vendor what you could get in your price range from someone else. You may not need to show a tangible copy of competitor pricing (though it can't hurt to have it available), but at least knowing that information will help you make a smart decision after negotiating with your top vendor.

The best way to start your negotiation is by getting the vendor excited to work with you. This doesn't mean being "fake" or insincere. When negotiating with the top vendors you want to hire for your wedding, show them your genuine enthusiasm for their products. If a florist knows she is your top choice, but her bouquet packages average $50 each above your budget, she may be willing to compromise out of flattery. Your appreciation for a vendor's work is also of value to them because you will be more likely to tell people about their services and leave good reviews after your wedding.

Another way of negotiating is to give the potential vendor a specific price reduction value to keep their services within your budget (e.g. $50 less per bouquet). This gives the vendor an idea what you can afford, and the opportunity to determine if reducing their price is still profitable for their business. Since they may try to meet you in the middle, you can always ask for a lower price than you actually need in hopes that "in the middle" will still be closer to your budgeted amount than their original pricing. Be open to the fact that they may not be able to reduce their prices as low as you need, at which point you have to decide if their services are worth re-arranging your budget, or if it would be best to go with your second choice.

You can also give the vendor the total amount you are willing to spend for that category of your budget, and then negotiate what "extras" you can get for FREE or at a discount if you spend that amount on their products/services. Your vendor may be able to create a discounted package to help you stay within your budget or throw in something extra that is not of huge expense to them, but gives you greater value for the price you are paying. For example, when the bridal shop cannot give you any additional discounts on your dress, ask what else they can offer you for FREE or at a discount to help you stay within your budget. They may be able to hook you up with some accessories or reduced alteration costs. If you don't ask for something, then the answer will definitely be no, so you might as well just ask.

While a reduction in price may be better for your budget, you need to be comfortable walking away from an offer if it doesn't feel right or isn't low enough for your budget requirements. If a price reduction also includes a reduction of services, make sure you receive a clear outline of what you are still getting for the new price you have negotiated. If the price fits your budget, but the value of the revised services doesn't meet your needs, then you may still want to consider going with another vendor.

Don't be phased by high pressure sales tactics. If you are offered a deal that you need time to think about it, chances are you will still be able to get that deal later. A vendor who wants your business will honor a promotion, even past its expiration (if possible). Depending on the type of vendor, some deals may actually be time sensitive, especially if they are offered as a corporate promotion.

When an offer is presented to you, ask how long it is available and who the decision maker is for that type of promotion (local manager, corporate office, etc.). This information will give you insight as to how much control the vendor has over the promotion, and allow you to separate a time sensitive deal from a high pressure sales tactic.

The more services you obtain from the same vendor/venue, the more negotiating power you will have. If you have your wedding at a hotel, you are not only renting out a reception room and possibly a ceremony room, but you are also likely contracting their vendors for catering and flowers as well as reserving a room block for your guests. That is a lot of potential income for that hotel from your wedding, so your ability to negotiate will be better there than with a venue or vendor whom you are only contracting for one type of service. As discussed in Tip #15, having a venue that gives you freedom can be more budget friendly, however, you may find that negotiating the packages with a venue that offers multiple services could end up working out better when you compare all of your options. This is another reason why doing all of your research before negotiating is so important.

Tip #28: Spread Out Your Expenses Over Time

As mentioned in Tip #1, there are many benefits to having a longer engagement. One key benefit is the ability to spread out your expenses over time. Saving for a wedding is much less overwhelming when your budget can be divided over a greater number of months. For a $12,000 budget, the idea of saving $500 per month for two years is a lot less intimidating than saving $1,000 per month for one year. More time = smaller monthly savings requirement = less financial strain = less stress = happy bride-to-be.

In addition to saving smaller portions of your budget each month, a longer engagement allows you to make smaller monthly payments (preferably on interest free plans) toward the bigger expenses in your budget. For example, let's say your venue cost is $4,000. The venue allows you to make a 25% down payment followed by as many additional payments as needed to pay in full, with the final payment due 90 days prior to your wedding. Since the remaining balance is $3,000, if the venue is booked 15 months before the final payment is due, then the monthly payments would only be $200. Budgeting for $200 per month will be much easier than making a $4,000 payment all at once.

Like the example above, other major wedding expenses can be broken down into smaller monthly payments, but this varies from one vendor to another. For example, when interviewing photographers, ask what payment plan options they have. This could be the pro/con that helps you choose between two comparable vendors. If a payment plan is available, you will likely be required to put down a deposit, however, having the flexibility to continue to save and make monthly payments on the balance is better than having to pay in full up front. You may also be required to make your final payment 90 days prior to when services are scheduled, so plan accordingly when you budget for that particular expense.

As mentioned in other tips, being able to shop around and compare prices is key to saving on your wedding expenses. In addition to payment plans, you can also spread your expenses out over time by focusing on purchasing smaller groups of expenses at one time. Designate one month for invitations, another month for wedding favors, and so on. Collect fun decor and centerpieces throughout your engagement - buying items as you find them (especially if they are on sale) - rather than rushing to find all of those pieces once you have saved up the amount you have budgeted for decor. Track those expenses and check to make sure you are staying within your budget as you shop over time. You can always adjust your budget if you find something early on that is perfect, but more expensive than what you originally budgeted.

Tip #29: Earn Extra Income and Incentives

While you've already read 28 tips to help reduce your costs, you may realize as you develop your budget that your current income will not be enough to cover the costs of your dream wedding. At this point, there are two ways you can consider increasing your budget: earn extra income or obtain funds in the form of credit cards and loans. Some couples may decide that they do not want to go into debt to pay for their wedding, so it is important to discuss this with your future spouse before even applying for credit or loans. There are a variety of ways to earn extra income, but think about how much time you can realistically invest into earning it on top of your current schedule, planning a wedding, and making quality time for your relationship (after all, that's the whole reason you are getting married).

Here are some ways to earn extra income:

1) Find a part-time job

    With the number of retail stores around, you are bound to find at least one that is hiring. Even just working seasonally would help add some cash to your wedding fund. If you can find a part time job that benefits your wedding budget in another way, it may be more worth your time.

Check out this list of potential employers and associated perks:

- Hotel: discounted employee rate to use for your honeymoon or friend/family rate to offer your out-of-town wedding guests
- Bridal Shop: discounts on dresses for you and your bridal party
- Salon: discounted or FREE beauty services
- Disney Store: complimentary park passes that could be saved for your honeymoon
- Restaurant or Bakery: discounts on food for not only your reception, but other pre-wedding events as well

While a part-time job is the easiest way to earn extra income, there are some downsides to this option as well:

- It may be difficult to find something compatible with your current schedule and other job(s)
- You may be required to work undesirable hours and/or holidays
- The hourly rate may be pretty low, especially compared to whatever other job(s) you currently have
- It may be difficult to request time off. In this case, you should definitely give your employer as much notice as possible about the important dates you need off due to

wedding events (e.g. bachelor/bachelorette party, bridal shower, rehearsal dinner and the actual wedding, of course).

2) Sign up with a direct sales business

Though there are usually some costs associated with starting a direct sales business, this option would give you the most flexibility when it comes to your earning potential and schedule. Pick a company that is already successful, offers products that you actual like and are passionate about, and has potential for profitable ROI in a short period of time. A direct sales company that offers a starter kit might be better than one that requires you to pay for a monthly membership; once you've made back the money spent on your kit, you are at least breaking even, and hopefully putting away profit toward your wedding fund. Research the training options available to give you the best opportunity for success. The last thing you want to do is invest in something that will drain your savings instead of build it for your wedding budget.

3) Sell your stuff

If you are not currently living with your fiancé, this is an excellent opportunity for you both to condense your belongings before combining everything together. While you can always have your own garage sale, you may have better luck selling your belongings in a community sale (check with your HOA or complex for these types of events) that brings in more shoppers. If you have good, quality photos of your items, utilize your social media sites to market them to your network as an alternative to websites like Craig's List (especially if you don't want to meet up with a stranger). Lastly, check out your local consignment stores, which will either pay a small amount up front or a larger amount after your item sells.

Here are some ways to make the most of utilizing credit cards:

1) Apply for a credit card with a lower introductory APR

There is an overwhelming number of credit card options available. Some companies will even offer 0% APR for the first 6 to 15 months of use, which would give you extra time to pay off your wedding debt without accruing interest on top of it. Research your options before applying and make sure you understand the terms and conditions. Most importantly, know exactly when your interest rate will go up so that you can pay your debt off before then, or be prepared for the new interest charges on your statement.

2) Earn rewards for your credit card purchases

There are a variety of credit cards with reward programs. If you want to use your rewards to help cover honeymoon costs, pick a card that offers travel credit. Many hotels and airlines have their own cards, and American Express has a card that gives you travel credit on your billing statement. You can also select a card that earns cash back equal to a percentage of what you spend. Use this cash to pay down your card debt or put it into your wedding fund for other expenses. When researching these options, read all of the details so you know exactly how the rewards are earned, when they will be available for use, what the requirements are to use them, and if they have an expiration.

3) Borrow a reasonable amount

Don't overcommit your financial capability. While getting a card with a $10,000 limit might seem like the easiest way to increase your budget, consider your ability to pay that off and how much interest you would be charged on top of the debt. Make a reasonable decision when it comes to your credit card limit or loan amount. Keep in mind that the amount of debt you have when you get married will not only affect you, but also your future spouse, especially in regards to major expenses like your ability to buy a house together.

One last piece of advice for this tip: be smart with any extra money that comes your way, including tax refunds, bonuses, and your lottery winnings (though playing the weekly lottery is not encouraged as a budgeting tip). In all seriousness, any unexpected money added to your wedding fund could reduce the number of hours you would spend earning the same amount or decrease the debt you are taking on to pay for your wedding. It could also give you the opportunity to have something that was originally out of your budget, so be sure to consider adding it to your wedding fund before spending it on something else.

Tip #30: Appreciate (But Do Not Expect) Financial Support

While having financial support from other people in your life can be very helpful, it is best to plan your initial budget without that funding, unless it is already in your possession. It is also important to avoid letting anyone convince you to purchase something more expensive than what you can afford, unless they are offering to pay for it. In this case, it is your responsibility to make sure everything is reserved, confirmed, and paid for within a reasonable amount of time, or you should politely decline and stick to what you budgeted for originally. This may sound harsh, but it is necessary to avoid a situation where you have made deposits or signed contracts, but that "promised" funding falls through and now you can no longer afford the venue and vendors you have booked. If you develop a realistic budget on your own, you will only commit to what you know you can afford, and you can always add extras or upgrades later if you have received additional financial support.

There are many pros to accepting financial support, but there are also some potential cons and questions to consider. Use the lists below to help assess whether or not it would be beneficial to accept financial support.

<u>Pros</u>

- Additional funding will help you reach your budgeted savings amount faster than saving on your own, so you may not have to earn as much extra income or take on debt. Plus, you will be less stressed about achieving your budgeted savings.
- You will be able to pay for things sooner, which may save you money. For example, some vendors and venues will give discounts for complete payment received far in advance of your wedding. You can also avoid using a credit card or signing up for a payment plan that would incur additional fees or interest.
- You can increase areas of your budget to afford more expensive options, such as a higher priced wedding dress, a more inclusive photography package, or additional flowers.

Cons/Questions
- The financial contributor may expect to have some decision making power based on the support they are offering.
- The financial support could fall through or be less than anticipated. Is the financial contributor reliable?
- How would you manage the situation if the funding is ultimately not received? Would there be time for a back -p plan?

If you feel comfortable with the potential cons and answers to those questions, then you are safe to accept the financial support. If not, then you should further evaluate the situation and either politely decline or have a back-up plan in case the expected funding falls through.

Hopefully the tips in this book will help you plan a budget that you can confidently rely on, while still encompassing everything you want for your dream wedding. It is up to you and your future spouse to decide if you are willing to go into debt to pay for your wedding, but with a realistic budget, you should be able to avoid that completely. Stick to your budget as much as possible, and updated it accordingly if changes occur, such as the final cost of an estimated expense (higher or lower than budgeted) or an adjustment to the amount of income for your budget (either by increase or decrease). Keeping an accurate budget will make the financial aspect of your wedding significantly less stressful, and allow you to focus on the fun parts of the planning process.

About the Author

Kimi Cunningham lives in Arizona with her soon-to-be husband, Stephen, and their Goldendoodle, Penny Lane. When she's not working one of her many jobs and businesses, Kimi enjoys taking dance classes, singing karaoke, going to the theatre, and watching baseball (Go Cubbies!).

Kimi is thrilled to have the opportunity to share her frugal ways with the world, and hopes you will continue to read her thrifty tips (on more than just wedding planning), by visiting lowbudgetbride.com and following @lowbudgetbride on social media.

Made in the USA
Lexington, KY
27 December 2017